Gospel Magic

How to Use Magic Tricks as Visual Aids

Andrew Thompson

Curate, Oakwood LEP, Derby

GROVE BOOKS LIMITED
RIDLEY HALL RD CAMBRIDGE CB3 9HU

Contents

Dedicated to my father and mother,
Captain Malcolm Thompson and Sister Nancy Thompson of Church Army.
Your love, faith and lifestyle have inspired me deeply.

The Cover Illustration is by Peter Ashton from an idea by Emma Stobbs
The Artwork is by Emma Stobbs

Church Army and the Grove Evangelism Series

Church Army has over 350 evangelists working in five areas of focus, at the cutting edge of evangelism in the UK. It co-sponsors the publication of the Grove Evangelism Series as part of its aim of stimulating discussion about evangelism strategies, and sharing experience of front-line evangelism. For further details contact: Church Army, Independents Road, Blackheath, London SE3 9LG. Telephone: 020 8318 1226. Fax: 020 8318 5258. Registered charity number: 226226

First Impression November 2001
ISSN 1367-0840
ISBN 1 85174 481 9

1
Introduction

There is an increasing interest in the use of magic tricks in evangelism. Today it is not unusual to see seminars and workshops being run on magic tricks as a visual aid for Christian ministers in theological colleges, and for children and youth workers as a part of their training courses. We see clergy and ministers in many different denominations, Church Army officers, Open Air Campaigners, Scripture Union workers, Salvation Army officers and missionaries all using magic tricks as a tool in their work of teaching and evangelism. In the following pages I want to commend the use of magic tricks as a viable and effective means of communicating the gospel.

With the declining church attendance statistics in the UK, the church is facing a constant challenge to find new ways of reaching out to different groups in the community. We offer here just one way of communicating the gospel which is visually stimulating, attention grabbing, has a wide age range appeal and which is incredibly flexible in the manner and context in which it can be used. Although none of the tricks and ideas in this book is unique, using these tricks in evangelism grew naturally out of my own use and performance. Other evangelists and Christian ministers have also come to similar conclusions and presentations of magic tricks, but to the best of my knowledge I have not used anyone else's routine or presentation directly.

In this booklet, we will be looking at a biblically-based theology of using magic in evangelism, and deal with some of the objections raised to the use of magic tricks in Christian ministry. We will look at some of the principles involved in magic tricks and then last but not least we will see some practical examples of how to do some tricks and use them in the context of Christian ministry.

One question frequently asked is 'Can anyone learn to do magic tricks?' What usually lies behind this question is an assumption that one needs to be incredibly dextrous and have the gift of the gab. My answer is that I believe anyone can learn to do tricks, regardless of speaking or physical ability (or disability—I myself am hearing-impaired and have a speech impediment). But when using magic tricks in public, like any other aspect of the performing arts, it is important to do them well. Nothing discredits Christian ministry more than sloppy, half-baked attempts to communicate with the public in any form of media. At the heart of any skill is the need to practise and practise. Finally, at the end of the book, if you are stimulated to develop further skills in this area then I highly commend the Fellowship of Christian Magicians. With regular conferences and a teaching magazine, they will encourage you and expose you to new ideas of proclaiming the gospel of Christ afresh to every generation.

2
Magic and Me

I am a Christian who is passionately committed to mission and evangelism. Over the years God has led me to many different places and placed me in different roles at home and abroad, from student to factory worker, missionary to youth worker and now to the ordained ministry in the Church of England. In all of these places and jobs, one common strand runs through my ministry and that is the use of magic tricks and other performing arts in order first to gain an audience and then to illustrate the gospel message.

When I took a year out with Church Army on a travelling faith-sharing team, I discovered the concept of Gospel Magic. I witnessed one Church Army officer (Captain Tony Maidment) holding young and old spell-bound as he preached and taught the Christian faith. To this day I never forget the impact of the things he taught, purely because of the way he used tricks and balloons to illustrate his message. From that time on I developed my own preaching ministry using the tricks which I had learned previously.

As a church-based youth-worker in the semi-rural area of Matlock Bath and Cromford in Derbyshire, I found that magic shows opened doors and ears during my ministry. Young people who were usually cynical about school assemblies and church services had their attention rivetted by the visual aids. During 1997 and 1998, I attended the Greenbelt Christian Arts Festival as a seminar/workshop leader in one of the 'Fringe' events and the high attendance at those sessions convinced me that people could see the potential of using magic in evangelism and preaching.

Today I am an ordained minister in the Church of England based at a Local Ecumenical Partnership church on the large estate of Oakwood in Derby. I continue to use magic tricks both to illustrate my messages and as a way of gaining access into groups in our community. In homes, hospitals, churches, youth clubs and outdoors, with young and old I find magic tricks a great 'ice-breaker' and way of leading into provoking and challenging dialogue about faith in Jesus Christ.

3
Magic in the Bible

One of the main concerns held by Christians about those who do magic tricks is that throughout the Bible the activity of magic is consistently condemned. It is important then to look at the biblical understanding of magic and contrast it with the kind of magic to which we are referring in the rest of this booklet.

Throughout the Bible, magic is described as the activity of sorcerers, magicians or wise men who used their knowledge to influence people and events. The magic they used was ritualistic and usually set within a cultic context.

Old Testament

K A Kitchen introduces us to the vocabulary of magic used throughout the Old Testament.[1] It is significant that the earliest books in the Bible use the Hebrew term *hrtm* which is derived from the Egyptian term for magician. Some of our earliest pictures of magic tricks come from the ancient Egyptians. The same Egyptian word can also be used for 'priest' thus emphasizing the strong link between magic and religion. In the book of Genesis this is the name given to those wise men and advisers in the court of Pharaoh who were asked by Pharaoh to interpret his dream. It was Joseph who made nonsense of their efforts by seeking this knowledge from God (Genesis 41). In the book of Exodus it was the same group of people who opposed Moses when he appealed to Pharaoh to let his people go (Exodus 7). These magicians were able to duplicate Moses' feats of turning his staff into a serpent, turning water into blood and producing frogs (Exodus 7.11, 7.22, 8.7). The account of this does not tell us if Pharaoh's magicians were able to accomplish this feat by supernatural occultic means or by devious trickery.

The other words used in the Old Testament referring to magic are tied with the practice and use of charms (Deut 18.11; Is 47.9), divination (Deut 18.10; Ezek 21.21), the use of herbs, and snake charming (Ps 58.5; Eccl 10.11; Jer 8.17). In the book of Daniel, the word *Kasdim* (Chaldean) refers to a class of people who had the role of magicians in the Babylonian court. We can infer from the stories told in Daniel that they were to advise the king, predict the future, and interpret dreams.

New Testament

In the New Testament the word *magos* is used to describe the 'wise men' of Matthew's gospel. Like *Kasdim*, the word Magi came to be used to describe a racial group in Media who were especially renowned for their knowledge in astronomy and astrology (hence the Magi following the star). The word *magos* is also used to describe those practising sorcery and magic in the book of Acts. It is from this Greek word we derive our own English word 'magic.'

1   K A Kitchen, 'Magic' in *The Illustrated Bible Dictionary* (Leicester: IVP, 1994) p 931.

Archaeological surveys of ancient magic practices describe activities which are often set in the context of a highly structured religious environment which is patronized by the ruling classes. Through the casting of spells, wearing of charms, and divination of the future, magic was seen as the main way to control the elements of both the supernatural and the natural world. The pagan gods were supposedly pacified through magic rituals and thus control was believed to have been exerted over the elements of the seas and winds and other natural forces.[2]

The Bible's attitude to these magic practices is outright condemnation. It is seen as a rival to true religion that undermines the sovereignty of God. The Bible explicitly forbids magic in Leviticus 19.26. Isaiah warns the people of Israel that despite their magic practices God will bring about his will (Is 47.9). It is the widespread use of magic in Israel which brings God's judgment. Even their rulers practised magic, for example Jezebel (2 Kings 9.22) and Manasseh (2 Kings 21.6).

The most explicit condemnation is in the book of Revelation where those who practise magic and deceive others are condemned in judgment along with idol worshippers and the sexually immoral (Rev 9.21, 18.23, 21.8, 22.15). In the book of Acts, there are various encounters with magicians and sorcerers and they are all overturned and rebuked by the work of the Holy Spirit (Acts 8 and 13).

In view of the Bible's teaching on the subject it is easy to see why there is a concern for any involvement in practices which involves magic or sorcery. There certainly is no biblical precedent for Christians to be involved with magic in good conscience. So how can we advocate the use of magic with evangelism?

The answer has to do with the nature of magic tricks described in this booklet. The problem is that the word 'magic' is an ambiguous term which is loaded with negative connotations linked with witchcraft, 'black and white magic,' the occult, voodoo, and so on. All of these things come under the type of magic which is rejected by Scripture as unacceptable to those who seek to please God.

So how can we justify using magic in Christian ministry? We need to demonstrate that the kind of magic that we do has *nothing to do* with the magic described in the Bible. The magic we do is not about appealing to pagan gods in order to influence people or events and we do not require people to believe that we hold supernatural powers. It is a form of entertainment in which people share the understanding that although they do not understand how the entertainer is accomplishing his or her feats they know it is by natural means as opposed to supernatural powers. Unfortunately, modern magicians often use occultic paraphernalia as a background 'dressing' for their act and this does mislead Christians into believing that their magic tricks are linked with the forbidden occult.

The word 'magic' is also widely employed to refer to the trickery used by skilful entertainers to create illusions and stunts in which they apparently defy the natural laws of physics in their feats. It is this aspect of the word 'magic' which we are now going to define.

---

2   For an illustrated insight into the magic world of the Egyptians see the work of F Lexa, *La Magie dans l'Egypte Antique*, 3 Vols (Paris: 1925).

4
A Definition of Magic

What do we mean by the word 'magic'? Henry Hay[3] defines magic as the 'art or game—of entertaining by tempting a particular audience to accept, temporarily, minor infractions of natural law.' And he suggests that these are mainly accomplished by manipulating the interest and perceptions of the audience. Through the use of mechanical apparatus, sleight-of-hand, misdirection (making the audience 'look the other way') and psychological associations, the entertainer is able to draw the audience into a world of make-believe where the impossible appears to happen.

A Brief History of Magic as an Entertainment Form
Quite when magic became distinct from religion as a form of entertainment is not known. What we do know is that it goes back a long way in human history. Edwin Dawes[4] suggests that the techniques of deception used by the Egyptian priests of pagan religions laid the foundations for a form of entertainment. He gives a fascinating account of some of the earliest records of magical performances found on tomb walls which described gruesome decapitation tricks. An ancient Egyptian magician called Dedi was able to cut off the heads of chicken, geese and other livestock and restore them back to life. Milbourne Christopher[5] also indicates that the Chinese had acrobats, jugglers and magicians in their courts at the same time as the Egyptians. Later on, during the time of Christ, we have evidence that there were entertainers who specialized in conjuring tricks as a form of entertainment. John Fisher[6] quotes the first century Latin philosopher, Seneca, who compared the politicians' rhetoric of the day as being the verbal equivalent of the sleight-of-hand used by the conjurers he saw in the market place. Obviously, some things never change!

Throughout the Middle Ages, troupes of 'jongleures' toured the great European markets and entertained the crowds with a wide variety of performing skills including magic tricks. Some were so good that they performed before royalty. Isaac Fawkes in 1720 records a visit of royalty to see his show in the Haymarket.

During the Victorian and Edwardian era, the music halls regularly featured acts by magicians. The gentry amused themselves by hosting 'parlour shows' in which entertainers were invited to give performances before a select audience in the drawing rooms of the wealthy. Robert Houdin, Maskelyne and Devant, Kellar, Chung Ling Soo and Harry Houdini all blazed trails as headline acts through the

3   H Hay, *The Amateur Magician's Handbook* (London: Signet Books,1983) p 2.
4   E A Dawes, *The Great Illusionists* (London: Chartwell Books Inc, 1979).
5   M Christopher, *The Illustrated History of Magic* (London: Robert Hale & Co,1973).
6   J Fisher, *Paul Daniels and the Story of Magic* (London: Jonathan Cape,1987).

1800s up to the 1920s. With the advent of television and film, magical entertainers were able to reach a far wider audience with their skills than ever before. In Britain, David Nixon and Paul Daniels popularized magic tricks through their own television shows. Today, magic is still a regular feature of television with several of the children's programmes presenters using magic as a way of connecting with their young audiences. One of these young presenters is Dominic Wood, who went on to present the children's series 'Animal Magic,' combining magic tricks with educational video clips about nature.

Today we can witness many forms of magic tricks, which are categorized by magicians into different groups. Close-up magic refers to tricks which can be done right under the noses of the spectators. Typically this might involve doing tricks with playing cards, coins and matchsticks. Then there is mentalism magic which involves the magicians pretending to predict the future or reading people's minds. The word 'illusion' is used by magicians in a very specific way. It refers to stage-sized tricks involving people or animals. Cutting a woman in half would be categorized by magicians therefore as an illusion. One of the up-coming forms of magic gaining a wide audience is street magic. The cool 'street-cred' of David Blane and others as they stop people on the street and reduce their street audience to screaming in disbelief at the effect of their magical tricks has just got to be seen.

5
Magic and Evangelism

Is there a biblical basis for using magic tricks in evangelism? Yes—*if* we understand that magic tricks are a kind of *visual aid*. More conventional visual aids in evangelism tend to include story telling, drama, pictures and using objects. Alongside these latter visual aids I would include magic tricks as being a legitimate means of illustration.

No-one knows for sure when magic tricks were first used as a visual aid for the gospel but we can look to both the Old and New Testament to see that God loved to use dramatic illustrations for his messages. The prophets of the Old Testament used vivid visual aids to dramatize Israel's relationship with God. From breaking pottery, going naked, burying soiled clothing, through to being tied up, there seems to be have been a no-holds-barred approach as to what they would do in order to gain a hearing for the 'word of the Lord.' Indeed, God himself communicated through dramatic signs. There was the whole business with Moses—appearing in a burning bush, turning a wooden staff into a snake, bringing various plagues on the Egyptians and then leading the Israelites through the parting of the sea and providing for them all through miraculous means. God's interaction with his people was dramatic and certainly not dull.

In the New Testament, Jesus continued communicating the message of God in visual ways. The parables drew on common images to illuminate spiritual truths. The dramatic healings, the exorcisms, the cursing of the fig tree were all means by which Jesus illustrated his message. There is a strong biblical precedent for the use of visual aids in communicating the message of God.

The use of magic tricks in preaching and proclaiming the gospel thus follows a biblical pattern in seeking to use dramatic ways to illuminate truth. Magic tricks, by their very nature, stimulate interest and intrigue and the element of surprise ensures that people go away remembering the encounter for a long time.

Truth and Method

One reason why magic tricks are effective visual aids today in Britain is to do with the belief that we are now living in a society which is described as 'postmodern.' One of the features that mark this society is a rejection of the notion of universal truth. The 'big picture' ideologies of science, communism and religion have been found wanting. The question which lies on people's lips is not 'What is truth?' but rather 'What is true to me?' When they explore other religions and ideologies they are making decisions based not so much on an objective rationale but on subjective experience. So they will be asking, 'Does this feel right or true to me?' Consequently they are interested in stories which illuminate individual experience. 'Out' is the desire and interest in theoretical explanations of the universe, but 'in' is the interest in personal and illustrated examples in which faith is revealed as something that 'works' for individuals.

This is where magic tricks can connect with today's audience. Combined as a visual aid with testimony, we will see the Christian message connect with our listeners. In one sense we have gone back to the original intention which lay behind Jesus' presentation of his message. He used visual aids not just to convey a new ideology or religion, but rather to expose each individual's need to encounter a God of salvation and forgiveness. The gospel stories show time and time again that Jesus met with individuals, and through the use of visual aids brought their needs into the open and offered opportunity for a personal and intimate encounter with God through the Holy Spirit. The story of the woman at the well illustrates Jesus' approach (John 4). I use this approach when sharing my own story of how I became a follower of Jesus by illustrating how I felt before my encounter with Jesus. I invite people to tie me up in handcuffs. Then I talk about the frustration I endured with my hearing impairment. I describe the sense of feeling trapped by the prejudices of others and my own sense of inadequacy. I visually and dramatically illustrate what Christ did for me when I escape from the handcuffs, explaining what I have been liberated from and how. This manner of storytelling will have far more impact than trying to explain the biblical truths of Christian freedom as an abstract idea.

As preachers we need to be aware that the majority of people grasp truth and ideas far more easily when they are presented in a concrete form. A quick survey of *The Sun* newspaper is a study of how news is presented in a concrete manner. News stories are usually illustrated with reference to an individual's experience and story. Contrast *The Sun* newspaper approach with that of the *Times* or the *Daily Telegraph* and you see a vast difference. The latter are much more theoretical and abstract in reporting a story. Using magic tricks in preaching makes truth become more accessible. It becomes a concrete illustration of something which, by its very nature, is abstract.

This is why the use of magic tricks in evangelism is so powerful, and why people who would not normally give the time of day to listening to a Christian message will stop and pay attention. It is because an abstract truth normally perceived as something which is beyond their interest is presented to them in a way that not only holds their attention because of its novelty but also enables them, perhaps for the first time, to engage clearly with the Christian message.

Objection!

So what are the problems in using this medium as a way of communicating the Christian message?

One objection I have encountered over the years is that magic tricks entail deception. As a people who are called to speak the truth, surely it is incompatible to use a means of deception to communicate truth. But although people may not understand how magic tricks work, there is no deception involved in as much as they know that the visual aid they have seen is a trick accomplished by clever natural means. We could argue that storytelling is deceptive for stories often call the listeners to enter into an imaginary world which is not real and so is therefore a falsehood. Yet we have no problem in using stories because people can use their imaginations to make a story illuminate truth. The critic will respond that everyone knows it is just a story and that they can make the distinction between fiction and non-fiction—but the same is true for magic tricks. People share an understanding that a magic trick is not 'real' but is a visual aid with a difference.

Another concern might be that because the use of magic tricks is so strongly linked with entertainment, the message of God is trivialized or even over-shadowed by the tricks.

The *Oxford English Dictionary* defines entertainment as a way of holding people's attention. Surely when we preach we want to hold people's attention? The tragedy is that often sermons do not hold people's attention, and despite the excellent and truthful content of the message, they are ineffective because people simply have not had their attention or interest gripped. This objection makes the assumption that somehow entertainment is not good, or at the very least it is seen as inappropriate for communicating truth. Some of the most powerful conveyors of truth have been from the entertainment industry. Countless Hollywood movies can inspire us, and affect us with their powerful portrayal of historical events and ideologies. Movies like *Ghandi, Cry Freedom, The Mission* and *Schindler's List* are all deadly serious in communicating the mistakes of history, and succeed far more successfully than a mere talk.

As for the use of magic tricks overshadowing the message, this can be true for any visual aid. We all know times when a good message has been flogged to death through the overuse of a visual aid. Care needs to be taken that the visual aid is appropriate and helpful in making a valid point.

For the parish minister who wants to break into new areas of his community, this is a skill, which can pay dividends. It is often assumed that this is something that only the 'children will like.' The truth is every generation is fascinated by magic tricks, and it has an almost universal appeal. I have performed in countries where the culture and language is far removed from my own, and my testimony is that magic tricks go down a treat there as well as here.

The Process of Discipling

Evangelism is the process by which one person encourages another to come closer to God. The 'Engel's scale' model of evangelism portrays the sometimes long process which people go through, before they come to full faith in Jesus Christ.[7] This model of evangelism reminds me that I have used magic tricks in situations which are decidedly pre-evangelistic contexts, right through to the moment when people make a profession of faith, and on through to the further stages of discipleship.

We now come to the real 'nuts and bolts' question. Can any busy parish minister learn magic tricks well enough to be able to use them in their ministry? The

7   J F Engel, *Contemporary Christian Communication, Its Theory and Practice.*

answer seems to be yes. Magic tricks are perceived to be very difficult to perform, and this is a perception which magicians are keen to foster! The truth is that the best magic tricks are in fact very simple to do. The real skill lies not in performing the mechanics of the trick but in presenting it in an engaging manner. Most ministers are used to speaking in public and so they are half way there to performing magic tricks! I have run seminars for colleagues in ministry and several of them have reported back to me with great pleasure the results of using the new skills they acquired through the seminars. They delight in the interest shown by normally inattentive audiences. They recall conversations in which people remember the messages illustrated with tricks long after the message was preached. Then of course, there is the deep satisfaction of pulling off a trick and baffling an audience, whether it be one or a hundred.

So where and how do we begin to develop the new skill of performing magic tricks? To this we now turn.

6

Getting Started

How does one begin to learn magic tricks? Is there a huge financial outlay in splashing out on fancy magic equipment? Does one need to begin finger gymnastics in order to gain the nimble digital dexterity required to pull off sleight-of-hand manoeuvres?

Let us start at the beginning. Do you feel that the use of magic tricks will enhance your own Christian ministry? First of all there must be a desire to learn and use magic tricks. Without that desire you will have stumbled at the first hurdle. Second you need to be committed to doing things well. Nothing is a greater turn-off than to see someone fumble or fluff their way through a performance. Thirdly we need to make sure that the trick serves the message rather than the message serving the trick!

The most effective tricks are those which are simple in method. The simplicity of how some tricks are accomplished can actually disappoint people. They were so completely taken in by the trick that they would expect a more sophisticated method to justify them being hood-winked! So consequently when you read the way in which a magic trick is accomplished, do not dismiss it out of hand because it seems to be too simple or obvious. All the tricks described in this book I regularly use with great effect and it is rare for people to guess the secret of the trick because they are looking for more complex solutions. Thus I encourage you to try out each trick as described in the next few pages one by one until you are proficient in performing them. Practise them on your spouse, sibling or close friend until they declare you are ready to be unleashed on an unsuspecting public!

When you read a magic trick 'text book' it usually follows a similar order of presentation in explaining and teaching how tricks work:

- *Effect.* The magic trick is described from the point of view of the audience. This is what it looks like or is supposed to look like and the effect you are trying to create for them.

- *Method.* This section then takes you back to the beginning of the trick and shows you step by step what you need to do in order to create the effect. Sometimes there will be a little check list which shows you what equipment you need to have ready before you begin practising the trick.

- *Presentation.* Some books leave this section out. But normally this would include the 'patter,' that is, the words you say and a story structure in which you present your trick. In this booklet I have called this section *Message*. This will give you the way in which I would present the magic trick in the context of a Christian message.

Having read carefully through the Effect, the Method and the Message, the next step is to practise. It is important that the 'mechanics' of doing the trick become second nature so as to allow you to focus on what you are saying with the trick. If the trick dominates the message then it defeats the point of the exercise. The point of the message should be the same as the point of the trick.

It may help you to write down in your own words what you would like to say (know your message) and practise in front of a mirror so you see what the audience will see. Finally, you need to be comfortable with your presentation, in that it reflects yourself. Do not try to be flashy, funny or frenetic if that is not your personality. Be yourself.

The following tricks have been selected for simplicity, their immediate application to a Christian message and their interest value to the audience. I hope you enjoy learning these tricks and find them useful. All the tricks mentioned use objects that can be found around the house, or are easy to make or purchase.

7

Gospel Magic for Beginners

1. Just Chance
Effect

A plate is displayed with several sealed envelopes on it and it is explained that one of the envelopes contains a twenty pound note. A game is played in which the audience can pick any envelopes leaving the last one for the magician. When the envelopes are opened, the audience discovers that theirs only contain blank, worthless slips of paper. The last envelope opened by the magician is seen to hold the twenty pound note.

Method

Place seven envelopes on a plate each one sealed with a blank piece of paper inside. Underneath the plate, place a twenty pound note which has been folded up small enough to be concealed by your hand holding the plate.

Offer the plate around explaining that you are going to play a game of chance and reveal that one of the envelopes has money in it. In fact a twenty pound note—would anyone like to play this game?!

With drama and humour allow all the envelopes, except for one, to be chosen and opened by members of the audience. Finally you take the last envelope off the plate and as you do so you slip the twenty pound note from underneath the plate to behind the envelope. The best way to do this is to have your right hand thumb on top of the envelope and your fingers underneath the plate concealing the twenty pound note.

Slide both towards you and ensure that the money is not seen by holding the envelope face towards the audience. Place the plate on a table, then open the top of the sealed envelope, reach behind the back of the envelope and pretend to pull out the money as though it were actually coming from inside the envelope. Immediately screw up the envelope with the blank piece of paper inside it and toss them away into a bin, leaving a twenty pound note on full display.

Message

We all make choices in life and I am going to invite you to make a choice right now which may richly benefit you. Inside one of these envelopes is a twenty pound note. There are seven envelopes and I am going to give you six chances to win the money. The last envelope left on the plate is mine.

(The six envelopes are opened and the blank pieces of paper revealed) Well what can I say? You all made the wrong choices and ended up with worthless bits of paper. Bad luck I guess or is it? My envelope contains the money. Here it is.

Jesus described the kingdom of God as being like a valuable pearl or treasure and that people gave up everything they had so they could purchase these precious things. What is precious to us in our lives? How do we make choices? St Paul told us that the most precious thing he ever did was to choose Jesus Christ to rule his life. He said that the choice he made in following Jesus Christ was worth more than anything else he ever did or owned.

(An alternative presentation to this trick would be to write down different life choices—fame, fortune, power, and so on—on all the blank pieces of paper and then for the final choice have a picture of Jesus or the cross concealed under the plate to pull out of your envelope. Thus you can talk about the different life choices that face us and talk through the different things written on the pieces of paper as they are revealed by members of the audience.)

2. The King of Hearts
Effect
The magician explains that in a copy of the Bible given to someone to hold in full view is a prediction made a few minutes before coming to speak to the audience. A volunteer is called out and chooses a card. The card is revealed. The Bible with the prediction in it is opened up to show that there is a playing card in it. The card in the Bible matches the one in the volunteer's hands...for they are both the King of Hearts.

Method
You need a pack of playing cards, an extra King of Hearts which is placed in a Bible. (I use a large sized playing card for the Bible so it is visible to a large group).

The secret of this trick lies in the ability to 'force' a volunteer to take the card that you want them to take. In this case the card you want them to pick is the King of Hearts. Before you meet your audience, go through the pack of cards and place the King of Hearts on top of the deck (when it is face up).

Call out a volunteer. Spread out the cards and quickly expose them to the volunteer explaining that there is a choice of 52 cards available in the pack.

Offer the pack to the volunteer and have them cut the pack of cards in half then take the bottom half, turn it 90 degrees and place it sideways on to the top of the upper half.

When this is done, the magician talks to the volunteer a bit about predictions, making choices and so on. This bit of patter is important because it is a distraction which is explained in a minute.

The volunteer is then asked to lift the top section of the cut cards and take the card off the top of the bottom half. (This is the King of Hearts. It was on top of the deck, then went to the middle as it was immediately beneath the cards that were placed on top of it at right angles.) Thus the King of Hearts ends up in the volunteer's hands. Although this is a very simple force, it is extremely effective as the time spent talking between the two cuts diminishes the memory of the fact that it is the original top card that is being offered.

The Bible is then brought forward and with much drama is opened to reveal the matching King of Hearts inside it.

Message

Is it possible to see into the future? Well I am going to have a go at predicting the future now. Earlier on I placed a prediction in this Bible which I am going to ask someone to look after. (Get a volunteer to hold the Bible firmly shut but in full view all the time.) Now in this pocket I have got a packet of cards and I would like someone to come out and help me. As you can see you have a choice of 52 cards and I would like you to cut the pack and place the bottom half on top at right angles. Would not it be just amazing if I could actually see into the future and see what is going to happen next even before it happens? Well this is what I am actually going to try and do with you right now. Would you like to lift up the top half of the pack and take the card that is underneath. Great! Now give me the rest of the pack and I will put it away. Have a look at your card and tell everyone what the name of your card is. Now let's see if the prediction comes true. (Bring the Bible forward and show the King of Hearts.) Wow, that's brilliant—my prediction has actually come true. Thank you for helping me.

Actually, as you know, this is just a clever trick. I cannot really see the future. However, I do know someone who can. In the Bible, God revealed through his prophets his plans for the future. These plans foretold the coming of Jesus thousands of years in advance. Everything that was revealed about the Messiah or the Suffering Servant came true in the person of Jesus Christ.

Even more scary is the thought that God has plans for us and he knows our future. He knows everything about us (Psalm 139). God loves us all so intimately he wants us to know that he is in control of our lives and that we can know our future for all eternity. He wants to be the King of our Hearts.

3. Eye of a Needle

Effect

A rope is twisted around a thumb and a loop is formed resembling the eye of a needle. Suddenly, without the end of the rope passing through the eye, the rope has 'magically' threaded itself through the eye of a needle in an instant.

Method

You need one metre of soft-core rope. Hold your right hand out as though you were going to shake somebody by the hand. Using your left hand lie the centre of the rope over the right hand thumb so that the ends of the rope are hanging down on both sides of the thumb. Pull up the end of the rope which is hanging down on the *outside* of the thumb and wind it around the thumb in a clockwise direction four times towards the tip of the thumb. Use the remaining bit of rope to form a loop. The important thing about this loop is that it is formed by lifting the

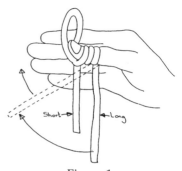

Figure 1

16

Figure 2

remaining bit of rope straight up and bending it over downwards to the right to form the loop, trapping the remaining length between the inside of the thumb and the fingers of the right hand (see figure 1).

Taking the other end of the rope with your left hand, you will discover that by gently pulling the end of the rope towards the left and then tugging upwards, between the thumb and the fingers, the rope will slide through the gap which is underneath the loop therefore appearing to be threaded through the 'eye of the needle.' Practise this movement until you can smoothly make the rope thread though the eye of a needle in an instant (figure 2).

Message

We often judge people according to their appearances and behaviour. Sometimes we feel that there is no chance for anyone to get into the kingdom of heaven just because we think that they are not the right type. In the gospel Jesus was approached by an ideal candidate. (Start winding the rope around your thumb). He was a rich young ruler. He had loads of money, was well respected and well connected. However, Jesus knew that the rich young ruler's heart was dominated by his wealth. So he told the young man that if he wanted to follow Jesus he must give away his wealth. The young man went away knowing that there was no way he was going to give up everything he had for Jesus. The disciples were upset and confused. If a nice rich guy cannot get into heaven then who can? At that point Jesus told them money could not buy God's favour. Indeed it 'was easier for a camel to go through the eye of the needle than for a rich man to get into heaven.' (Make the eye of the needle with the rope loop.)

This provoked the disciples to ask 'Who then can get into heaven?' Jesus replied 'What is impossible for man is possible for God.' (Pull the rope up through the eye of the needle). The good news is that no one can get into the kingdom of heaven on their own merit. It is only through Jesus that we can do this and so anyone who comes to God through Jesus will go through 'the eye of the needle.'

The Changing Bag
Effect

This is a prop which can be used for several different tricks and effects. The following gives you an idea of the some of the tricks you can do with it.

a) A dirty hanky is placed into a bag, after a moment the bag is turned inside out to reveal a sparkling clean hanky.

b) A rope is cut up and placed into the bag and when it is turned inside out, the rope is seen to be restored to one length again.

c) Three separate different coloured handkerchiefs are placed in the bag and when it is turned inside out they have all knotted together into an endless circle.

Method

You can make changing bags from plastic shopping carriers, paper bags, newspaper and so on—but for a nice prop that will last a long time it is best to use a soft, thick cloth material. Mine is made out of thick cotton material.

Cut out three pieces of identical coloured material measuring 30 cm long and 20 cm wide. Place them on top of each other and square them up. Then stitch up the two long sides and one short side to create a bag which has a dividing partition inside it (see figure 3).

Figure 3

What happens during the trick is simple. You place one article inside one side of the bag and simply take out another article which is concealed on the other side. For example in the trick where a dirty hanky changes into a clean one, the method is as follows. Before you show the trick to anyone you have secretly placed the clean hanky inside one of the partitions in the bag. To begin the trick, you show the bag empty by turning it inside out to reveal the empty partition. It helps to roll the top edges of the bag over thus concealing the extra pocket. The dirty hanky is then placed inside the empty partition of the bag and while you are talking, your fingers pull the dividing cloth over to the other side so that you can gain easy access to the clean hanky. Once again you reverse the bag inside out revealing the clean hanky to the audience. The dirty hanky is now concealed on the other side of the partition.

The same method exists for the other effects described above except of course the complete rope is concealed in the bag while you cut up another rope and place the pieces into the other side of the bag. The knotted circle of hankies likewise are placed in the bag before the show and are switched for the separate hankies which are placed into the other side of the bag one by one.

Message

a) Isaiah once displayed a dirty pair of linen shorts to tell the people that was how God saw their sins. In the Bible, God describes our lives as being like filthy rags. (Display the dirty hanky). When we put our trust in Jesus however, the Bible describes a transformation. Our dirty rags are exchanged for shining, sparkling clothes of righteousness. (Reveal the clean hanky and turn the bag inside out to reveal its emptiness).

b) We often talk about broken relationships. (Display the rope). The Bible describes how sin breaks our relationship with God. Every time we lie, hurt people or simply ignore God, our relationship is severed because our God is perfect. (Cut up rope and place the pieces into the bag). Jesus Christ came to this world in order to restore our broken relationships with God and if we come to God through Jesus and say sorry for the things we have done wrong then our relationships with God are mended and made whole. (Turn bag inside out to reveal the complete rope).

c) The Trinity is such a hard thing to explain. It is important for us to understand that the Bible reveals three separate persons who are God. There is God the Father, God the Son and God the Holy Spirit. (Display the three hankies and place them one by one into the bag). One time in the Bible where we read of all three persons being revealed at the same time, was when Jesus allowed himself to be baptized by John the Baptist. When he came up out of the water, the Holy Spirit descended on Jesus in the form of a dove and a voice spoke from heaven declaring 'This is my son in whom I am well pleased.'

Later on Jesus reveals that he and the Father are one and that the Spirit who will come after him was also part of them as well. So the three persons all link up to make one God. (Display the knotted hankies). They are equal but are seen in different roles. They are separate but are joined together as one.

The Compass
Effect
A square card is shown with an arrow displayed on it. As the card is spun round by the corners, it is seen that there is another arrow on the other side which is pointing in the opposite direction. During the talk and without warning, suddenly the arrows are pointing the same way. After that there is a bewildering change of directions and as the talk progresses, once again the arrows are seen to be pointing the same way.

Method
Needed is a square sheet of stiff thick card (or alternatively plastic or wood). The size can vary but a decent size is 20 cm by 20 cm. Begin by decorating the card by painting both sides the same colour. Then cut out two arrow shapes from sticky-backed paper. Make sure that the colour of the arrows contrasts with

Figure 4

the colour of the background of the rest of the card so that they can be seen clearly. The first arrow is placed on one side of the card pointing upwards vertically. The second arrow is placed on the other side of the card pointing horizontally to the side. In other words they are set at right angles to each other.

Hold the square compass diagonally by opposite corners and spin around to display both sides to the audience. Make note of the directions in which the arrows are pointing. If the arrows are pointing the same way, put a little dot in the corners you are holding to remind you of how to hold the compass if you want the arrows to point the same way. Now swap corners. This time you will see the arrows pointing in different directions.

I do not understand the physics of this trick; all I know is that the arrows point in different directions according to which corners they are held by. This trick is practically self-working. So according to your story line, display and spin the board to reveal the arrows pointing the same way or different ways as appropriate.

Message

Jesus described himself as 'the Way.' In fact the early Christians were known as followers of the Way. (Display arrows pointing the same way). The Bible reveals that God wants people to find the way to himself. It is in Jesus that we can discover a personal relationship with God. Jesus said 'I am the only way...' If we look at God's compass we see that the arrows are all pointing the same way.

Now God could have made us like robots where we would have no choice in knowing which way we were going. But because God wants a love relationship with us he gave us a choice. We could choose God or choose our own way. (Show the arrows now pointing in different directions). God's love for us stretches as far as the West (hold the card in right hand and point arrow horizontally to the right), all the way to the East (point arrow to the left using left hand), as high as the heavens above (stretch up and point the arrow upwards), and as low as the earth below (point arrow downwards). If we want to discover God's love for us, then we need to make our own choice in which way we walk. Do we go God's way or our way? (Spin arrows in different directions). Ultimately though, God wants everyone to know him and he hopes that we can all know him through Jesus Christ who said 'I am the way, the truth and the life.' (Spin arrows in the same direction).

The Thumb Tip
Effect

A silk handkerchief is placed in the hand. When the hand is opened the hanky has completely disappeared. Waving the hands around mysteriously the silk hanky suddenly reappears back inside the hand.

Method

You need a 'thumb tip' which can be bought in a novelty or joke store for less than two pounds, and a silk hanky which is nine inches square. A thumb tip is basically a hollow, flesh coloured tube of plastic designed to fit on top of your thumb. Used properly it is practically invisible except to the knowing eye. Like the changing bag, the thumb tip can be used for a variety of different tricks. We use silk because it can be compressed into a small space and when released it instantly expands to its original size again.

Before you begin to do this trick place the thumb tip on your right hand thumb (see figure 5). The silk hanky is then displayed between finger and thumb of both hands. Next you curl your right hand fingers into a loose fist. While you are preparing to tuck the hanky with your left hand into the hole in your fist, you secretly insert your thumb tip by sticking your thumb inside your fist and withdraw it leaving the thumb tip behind (see figure 6). The left hand drapes the silk over the right hand so that the centre of the hanky is above the tip concealed in the fist. Using your left hand forefinger poke the hanky into your fist but actually you are pushing the hanky into the thumb tip.

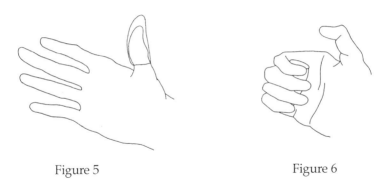

Figure 5   Figure 6

Use your left thumb to 'steal' the thumb tip by pretending to poke the hanky further into the right fist (see figure 7). As soon as the thumb tip is withdrawn from the right hand continue to poke into the empty fist with your left hand finger for a couple of more times so that the audience does not know or realize that anything has happened. Keep the thumb tip hidden discretely behind the cover of your left hand. Move your right hand towards the audience and slowly unfurl your fingers to show that the hanky has disappeared.

To reveal the hanky again, close your right hand again into a fist and pretend to reach inside it with your left thumb. Pull the hanky out by gripping the thumb tip inside your fist with your right fingers and pulling the hanky out with your left thumb into full view of the audience. While they are looking at the hanky quietly slip your right hand thumb into the thumb tip and place it in your pocket at an appropriate time.

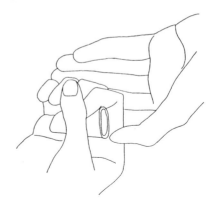

Figure 7

Message
One of the biggest mysteries in all time is the empty grave of Jesus Christ. For other religions we can go and visit the tombs where the bodies of their founders lay. In Christianity we can only visit an empty tomb. So what happened to the body of Jesus Christ?

History tells us that Jesus existed (display hanky) and that he was a very controversial character. He made claims that he was God. He healed the sick, gave life to the dead and cast out demons. History tells us that he was tortured by the Romans and then crucified to death on a cross. (Stretch out the hanky between your hands). The followers of Jesus came and placed his dead and broken body into a dark, cold tomb. (Place hanky into the thumb tip and do the 'steal'). A heavy stone was rolled over the tomb and a military guard was placed on duty to ensure that no-one moved the body. For two days Jesus laid in the tomb and then on the third day some women came to clean and wash the body as was their custom. They found the stone had been rolled away and that there was no dead body inside (unfurl your fingers to show that the hanky has disappeared).

There have been many theories of what happened to the body of Jesus, but the Bible tells us that for several days afterwards the disciples met, talked with and ate with Jesus who was alive after being killed. This had such a profound impact on the followers of Jesus that they practically turned the world upside down. So where is Jesus now? The Bible tells us that he is now ruling in heaven at the right hand of the Father and that through his Spirit we can come to know him in our hearts and lives. (Reach into your closed right hand above your heart and pull out the hanky). If you want to know where Jesus is today—I challenge you to ask him into your life and discover that he is alive today.

8
Conclusion

This booklet has demonstrated that it is possible to use magic tricks in Christian ministry as a visual aid. By providing some examples of magic tricks which lend themselves to a Christian message I hope that you are equipped to begin the first steps of using this medium as a feature of your own ministry.

Magicians are encouraged to keep the secrets of their tricks to themselves. There are several reasons for this. The first is that it simply defeats the point of the visual aid if one immediately explains how it is done. Secondly, the audience do not want to know how the trick is done. The reaction of the audience when they are told the secret of a trick is usually disappointment, as they like the challenge of having to work things out for themselves. Once they are told how the trick is done this leads to loss of interest and occasionally annoyance that they had been taken in so easily. One motto in the Fellowship of Christian Magicians is 'Keep the secret, share the word.'

Finally it is worth pointing out that magic has closely related allies which equally lend themselves to evangelism. These include the exciting and dramatic art of escapology, balloon modelling , juggling and puppetry, the last of which can involve the art of ventriloquism. All of these related performing arts can be explored through some of the books and dealers mentioned below.

9
Going Further

If you are wanting to develop your interest and skills in performing magic tricks as part of your ministry, then one of the first ports of call should be the Fellowship of Christian Magicians (FCM). The parent body for this organization is in the USA, but there is a European branch which is largely based in the UK. The address is:

Fellowship of Christian Magicians (Europe)
Secretary: Mrs Joyce Mabb, 28 St Giles Close, Church St Holme, Peterborough PE7 3QZ

They also have quite an extensive website which offers link pages to other related areas of interest. The email and website are cyber-fcm-subscribe@fcm.org and www.fcme.co.uk

Dealers of Gospel Magic
Selling magic tricks is a very specialized business, especially if you are selling magic tricks specifically to magicians who want to use them as part of their Christian ministry. Below are some dealers who run mail-order catalogues for Christian magic and the best thing to do is write or call for their latest list.

Tricks for Truth
91 Green Street, Middleton, Manchester M24 2T3
Tel: 0161 653 6626

The FCME Store
Reg Heasley, 3 Turner St, Barnoldswick BB18 6AT
Tel: 01282 816002

Other Dealers
Of course not all dealers specialize in Christian ministry and the dealers listed below offer a wide and extensive range of magic tricks which range from small coin tricks right up to large-scale illusions of making people disappear or levitate.

International Magic Studio, 89 Clerkenwell Rd, London EC1R 5BX

Davenports Magic, Charing Cross Underground Shopping Concourse
The Strand, London WC2N 4HZ

Repro Magic
46 Queenstown Rd, London SW8 3RY
Tel: 020 7720 6257

Magic Books by Post
29 Hill Avenue, Bedminster, Bristol BS3 4SN
Telephone orders or Fax 0117 977 4409

A Short Bibliography
Some useful books which I recommend as an introduction to gospel magic:

H Smith, *Colourful Gospel Magic* (Taunton, 1988) and *Simple Gospel Magic with Economy Props* (Taunton, 1987)
K Wills, *Now You See It* (Carlisle: Alpha Books, 1999)
D Wilson, *12 Gospel Tricks with Money* (Owasso: Dock Haley, 1988) and *12 Gospel Tricks with Thumb Tip* (Owasso: Dock Haley, 1986)

(H Smith's and D Wilson's books are available from Tricks for Truth)

For more general books on magic which will teach you tricks without the Christian message, I can recommend the following:

P Eldin, *Pocket Book of Magic* (London: Kingfisher Books, 1990)
B Murray, *Paul Daniels Adult Magic* (London: Michael O'Mara Books Ltd, 1989)
P Page, *The Big Book of Magic* (London: Book Club Associates, 1976)

Finally, a really good way of learning magic tricks is through the use of videos. You can get a list of videos from the magic dealers mentioned above. The videos are useful for seeing what the trick is supposed to look like to its audience and then seeing how it is done step by step. It is easier than having to follow complex typed instructions.